Trumpet the Miracle Wolf Pup

Trumpet Grows Up

By Leokadia George

Illustrated by Maddy Moore

Briley & Baxter Publications | Plymouth, Massachusetts

ISBN: 978-1-954819-47-4

Book Design: Stacy Padula

This book is dedicated to Katie and Cristina,
Through forests and up mountains we run with wolves and
dragons, catching our dreams along the way.

This story portrays the life of Trumpet, F1505 a Critically
Endangered Mexican Gray Wolf, and was inspired by true
events at the Wolf Conservation Center.

On a chilly day at the Wolf Center in New York, Trumpet the Miracle Wolf Pup was snuggling with her mother inside their den. She was too young to see or hear anything, but she could feel her mother's warm fur and knew she was loved.

As she turned two-weeks old, her eyes started to open so she could finally see her mom. She looked around and noticed other things as well. What caught her attention most was the bright light coming from the front of the den. It made her very curious. She slowly crawled towards the opening, and all of a sudden, she saw a whole new world of green grass, tiny flowers, and gigantic trees.

As Trumpet stepped outside of her den, she could hear all sorts of new sounds. She heard lots of chirps from all the birds and the buzzing sounds from the insects.

Suddenly there was a sound that made her ears perk up right away. She heard a deep and lonely howl off in the distance—and not a howl from her mother or father.

One wolf's lonely howl led to another wolf's howl... and then another!

Just then, Trumpet's mother started howling, and her father joined in as well.

With all the wolves howling together, Trumpet found the courage to howl with the group. She lifted her head up took a deep breath and let out her loudest howl yet. Her voice was much higher than her parents' voices, but all the different howls flowed together in perfect harmony.

She did notice a couple other high-pitched howls off in the distance, which made Trumpet think, Could it be that there are some other small wolf pups out there?

Since she was the only small wolf pup in her family, she would spend her days exploring by herself, trying to catch the frogs hopping away or chewing on a nice stick. However, the most fun of all was trying to chew on her dad's ears!

Trumpet was getting bigger and faster, but growing up can still be tricky sometimes. The ground would suddenly change from soft grass to hard rocks.

One time, she even lost her footing on a hill and went tumbling down all the way to the bottom.

She finally stopped rolling and stood up—a little bit dizzy but she was okay. She learned to be more careful around those wet rocks on the hill!

As the weeks turned into months, her senses became stronger. Her ears could pick up sounds from very far away.

Every once in a while, she heard a very strange type of howl. It started off really high and then it got low, and it alternated going from high to low over and over again.

Trumpet was very curious to find out what kind of wolf made such a strange howl!

As Trumpet continued to grow, her nose grew longer, and she was able to smell many new scents. She could sniff the ground to discover who had traveled there recently—a chipmunk and those funny frogs!

She would even come across some real interesting scents, like that brown thing along the fence...

Oh! That is Mommy's poop!

Trumpet's eyes had changed color from blue to green, and she was starting to see the world much better—especially at dusk or dawn, when the sun was setting or rising. Those were the times when all the wolves loved to howl and play.

On a rare occasion, she noticed a strange, two-legged creature, walking by outside of her home.

Her mom and dad would get scared when this creature came around, often running in the other direction. Trumpet decided it would be a good idea to run away as well!

Early one morning, a large group of those two-legged creatures came into her enclosure!

Trumpet and her parents were very scared, so they ran away to hide. However, Trumpet's hiding spot was not very good, so she was found rather quickly.

The curator, who was in charge of keeping all the wolves healthy at the center, put on thick gloves and picked up scared little Trumpet to bring her to the very box where she was born. Trumpet was about to get her very important, three-month health check!

Then the curator brought her out again and held Trumpet steady while the veterinarian used a strange tool with a bright light to look into her eyes and ears. Then she even checked her teeth! They pricked her with something sharp, but she was so scared she barely felt it.

Trumpet was a very healthy, three-month-old pup, and everyone was happy—except scared, little Trumpet, who missed her mom and dad.

Just then, Trumpet was lifted off of the exam table and put back on the ground in her enclosure. She was confused and still a bit scared, but suddenly she realized she had the chance to run away from all the people. So, she did just that!

From her new hiding spot, she could see all the people leave her enclosure. Now she knew it was safe to look for her parents.

Of course, her parents knew the people left, so they were looking for her, too.

As they finally spotted each other, they ran towards one another, jumping, giving kisses, and howling in celebration! They were one happy family again!

The End.

Acknowledgements

  The Wolf Conservation Center is a 501c3 nonprofit environmental education organization committed to conserving wolf populations in North America through science-based education programming and participation in the federal Species Survival Plans for the critically endangered Mexican gray wolf and red wolf. Through wolves the WCC teaches the broader message of conservation, ecological balance, and personal responsibility for improved human stewardship of our world. For more information, visit www.nywolf.org.

Featured In This Story

- F1505 aka Trumpet
- M1059 aka Diego (Trumpet's father)
- F1143 aka Rosa (Trumpet's mother)
- Rebecca Bose (curator at the Wolf Conservation Center, who cares for all the wolves that reside there)
- Spencer Wilhelm (director of operations at the Wolf Conservation Center, who is in charge of construction and maintenance as well as assisting with animal care)
- Dr. Renee Bayha, DVM (has graciously volunteered her veterinary services to the Wolf Conservation Center since 2001)

CPSIA information can be obtained
at www.ICGtesting.com
Printed in the USA
LVHW071921201122
733506LV00014B/353